FIFTEEN LYRICS

FIFTEEN LYRICS

by

Joseph Moncure March

London

MMXIX

First printed in 1929
The Fountain Press, Inc.

CONTENTS

I.

FROZEN

Forever and ever this wind will toss
Black branches against a bleak sky:
And the harsh, white snow will whisper and sift
Endlessly till the day I die

Forever and forever I shall sit
And stare with changeless eyes of ice:
And frost will decorate my flesh
With many a strange, fragile device.

Forever my heart will know the peace
That comes only when the heart is frozen.
Live with ice, or live with fire:
So it was offered: and I have chosen.

II.

COULD IT BE I?

Could it be I who once bent over
To watch a bee balancing on clover?
Could it be I who lay in sweet
Grass watching far hills shimmer with heat:
Or I who walked with drunken tread
Staring at swift clouds overhead?

I think some other person must
Have bathed hot hands in the cool dust
That lay at twilight by the rutted road's
Blurred edge: been startled by a toad's
Long leap from shadow into shadow:
And stood tear-blinded by a slow
Darkening world, filled with the brusque
Husky singers of the dusk.

No one of that sort could have grown
This fond of flesh, and steel, and stone.

III.

SNOW KISS

Those whose hearts have known the cold
Kiss of snow, unloose their hold
On burning flesh. The kiss slips
A veil of ice over their lips,
Sealing them against the sweet
Puckered mouths that blossom heat.
They get glittering, cold passions
That must be sought in other fashions.

They walk alone, staring through dim
Frosted eyes at black slim
Branches etched against the white
Sparkling snow. They spend the night
Listening to the wind's wail,
And the swift, staccato hoofs of hail:
Waiting to see sharp-edged metallic
Moons set shadows in blue italic.

When these people brood, their dreams
Are like slow, dark, ice-covered streams
Marbled by strangely twisted flaws;
Hieroglyphed by birds' claws.

Finally they stiffen. They sit numb,
Waiting for a Spring that does not come.

IV.

BROKEN

Yes, I suppose some time I may
Throw these broken bits away;
Or bind them with cement and string
Into some cracked and hideous thing —
Which in due course I doubtless will
Point out to show my mending skill.

But now I stand with trembling lip,
Wishing I had not let it slip.

V.

BITTER MOOD

I have lived with the grim oak
And the savage, black pine
There is no meekness in their hearts,
And not any in mine.

Proudly I shall go to destruction;
Haughtily I shall fall.
The worms that come to taste my corpse
Will spit it out like gall.

VI.

RESURRECTION

Not even Spring can raise the dead
Painlessly. The slow spread
Of sap through a frozen tree's
Veins must bring agonies.
Just as savage blood retuning
To frozen flesh sets it burning:
Just as passion stirring again
Thaws a frozen heart to pain:
Just as slow recurring dreams
Torture a frozen head to screams.

But who considers pain objection
Enough to forego resurrection?

VII.

WINDY SPRING DAY

Clouds drag swift shadows over earth.
The light quivers with silent mirth.
Leaves shimmer like green mist;
Flash in the wind, sun-kissed.
Dust glimmers: Stone gleams:
The hawk flaps: the eagle screams:
Cherry blossoms, drenched in scent,
Nod and wink their merriment.

If Death himself should come to-day,
He would be beautiful, and gay.

VIII.

AFTER GRIM BURIAL

After grim burial, once in so often
I shall awake inside my coffin.
I shall lie staring upwards toward
The close lid, and be vastly bored.
And one day when the low hills burn
Yellow and crimson, I shall return.

I shall pluck off the rotted wrap
And brush the worm dust from my lap:
Press up against the lid with bone-
White hands until the red nails groan
And bend, twisting in agony,
Finally letting me go free.

I shall live one autumnal day
In some strange, half-remembered way.
Then, having had enough of pain,
Tired, I shall lie down again
With bright leaves rustling in my skull
To make death's sleep more beautiful.

IX.

CHARITY

Last night a thin wind
Snuffed at my palms,
And whined like a beggar
Asking for alms.

So I took out and tossed him
An old letter
Which he carried off,
And we both felt better.

X.

SUDDEN STORM

Under the seed of rain sowers
The streets burst into crystal flowers.
Papers flap torn, white
Wings in bewildered flight.
Black mushroom shapes walk
Each on a human stalk.
The sowers pass. The crystal crop
Vanishes. The fungi drop.
Strange fragrance is the sole token
Of enchantment made, enchantment broken.

Curtain. After a brief pause
Distant thunder stamps applause.

XI.

NOCTURNE

Silence. But the dark stirs
Uneasily. Like golden burrs
Lamps cling with slender bright
Barbs on the cloak of night.
Around the lamps, pale green
Leaves droop. Unseen
Blossoms throw a fine snare
Of fragrance on the still air.
With notes like opening flowers
Slow bells chime the hours.
Presently graves will yawn
And skeletons will walk till dawn.

XII.

ROCK

Who has a key that can unlock
The awful mystery of rock?

My body creeps: my blood runs chill
Before a thing so cold and still:

A thing so utterly alone
It's very dreams must all be gone:

A thing that holds the air of doom
Whether in statue, cliff, or tomb:

That views my world of mind and sense
With horrible indifference.

I have a feeling it is good
Rock cannot speak of what it would.

XIII.

AUTUMN PROPHECY

The dead leaves dance like withered witches;
Teetering, swirling
Drooping and curling
And crackling in the dried up ditches.

Hear them whisper as we go past:
How each dry lip
Rustles gossip!
Do you hear them saying our love won't last?

XIV.

PARTING

I wonder what passionate farewell
These petals took from the stiff stem:
With what reluctant grief they fell
Into the grass surrounding them.

XV.

CITY AUTUMN

The air breathes frost. A thin wind beats
Old dust and papers down gray streets,
And blow brown leaves with curled-up edges
At frightened sparrows on window ledges.
A snow-flake falls like an errant feather:
A vagabond draws his cloak together,
And an old man totters past with a cane
Wondering if he'll see Spring again.

ABOUT THE AUTHOR

Joseph Moncure March (1899-1977) was the first managing editor of *The New Yorker*, and helped create the magazine's *Talk of the Town* section. After leaving the magazine, March wrote the first of his two important Jazz Age narrative poems, *The Wild Party*. In 1928 he followed it up with *The Set-up*. Moving to Hollywood in 1929 he became the script writer who turned the silent version of Howard Hughes' classic *Hell's Angels* into a talkie — a rewrite that brought the phrase *"Excuse me while I put on something more comfortable"* into the American lexicon. A screenwriter in Hollywood until 1940 he eventually became a writer of documentaries for the State Department and a feature writer for *The New York Times Magazine*.

www.ingramcontent.com/pod-product-compliance
Lightning Source LLC
Chambersburg PA
CBHW031927090426
42811CB00002B/110